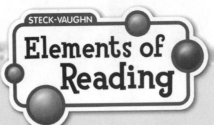

Vocabulary

Isabel L. Beck, Ph.D., and Margaret G. McKeown, Ph.D.

Writer's Log

Illustrations

Eldon Doty

Photography

Additional photography by Dover Publications, Dynamic Graphics, PhotoDisc/Getty Images, Cindy Aarvig/SV, Darcy Tom/Rigby, Corbis Royalty Free.

Steck Vaughn™

A Harcourt Achieve Imprint

www.Steck-Vaughn.com
1-800-531-5015

ISBN 1-4190-3049-3

Hello!

This Writer's Log is a place for you to use some new and exciting words in your writing. Some of the words might be a challenge to learn. But once you learn them, they will help you say exactly what you mean!

Now, let the writing begin!

CONTENTS

spirited	A spirited action is one that shows great energy and courage.

David wanted his dance to be more spirited, so

contract	If something contracts, it pulls together or becomes smaller and shorter.

The rubber band contracted quickly when

impulse	An impulse is a sudden desire to do something.

The last time I did something on impulse was when

arresting	Something that is arresting grabs your attention so much that you stop what you're doing.

The actor had such an arresting voice that

composure	Someone with a lot of composure appears calm and controls their feelings, even in difficult situations.

Tamara always keeps her composure, except

infer	If you infer that something is the case, you figure out that it is true based on what you already know.

When Betsy was absent, her coach inferred that

perceptive	A perceptive person is good at noticing or realizing things that are not obvious.

My father is very perceptive because

refute	If you refute something, you prove that it is wrong or not true.

Cameron refuted Jonna's argument by

- ☐ **spirited**
- ☐ **contract**
- ☐ **impulse**
- ☐ **arresting**
- ☐ **composure**
- ☐ **infer**
- ☐ **perceptive**
- ☐ **refute**

How Many Words Can I Use?

And still make sense!

Write about what you read in "Livin' on the Edge."
What's the most exciting thing that you have done?
What happened? Use as many words as you can.
Have fun, but make sense!

Word Wiggle

Fill in the boxes around the word wiggle with the vocabulary word that best fits each clue. The first one has been done for you.

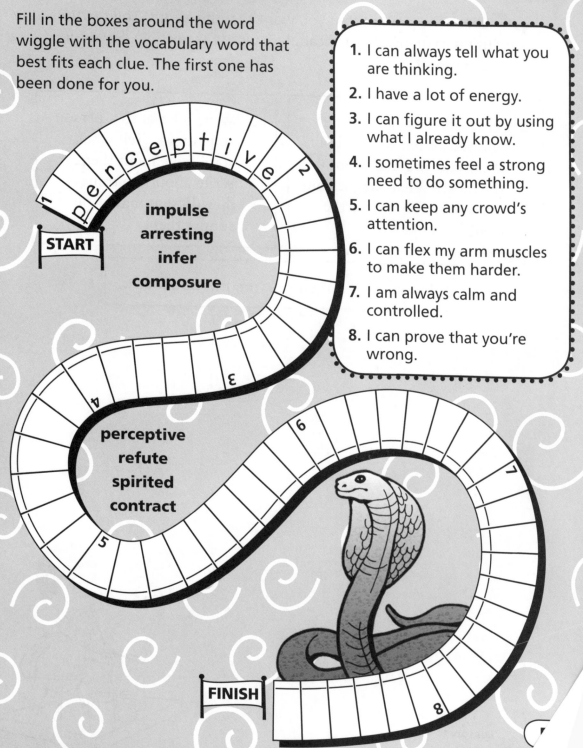

START

p e r c e p t i v e

1

2

impulse
arresting
infer
composure

3

4

perceptive
refute
spirited
contract

5

6

7

FINISH

8

1. I can always tell what you are thinking.
2. I have a lot of energy.
3. I can figure it out by using what I already know.
4. I sometimes feel a strong need to do something.
5. I can keep any crowd's attention.
6. I can flex my arm muscles to make them harder.
7. I am always calm and controlled.
8. I can prove that you're wrong.

In My Own Words

Check the prompt that you want to write about. Then write a story using as many of the vocabulary words as possible. Have fun, but make sense!

☐ Think of a book that you enjoyed. What was it about? What did you like about it the most? What caught your attention? What were the characters like?	☐ Write a letter to a person you admire. Tell what you know about them. Write about the things they do that make you admire them.

☐ Think of your own story and write about it.

These are the words I used!

- [ ] spirited
- [ ] contract
- [ ] impulse
- [ ] arresting
- [ ] composure
- [ ] infer
- [ ] perceptive
- [ ] refute

TOTAL WORDS USED

7

Take It Further

| undulate | If something undulates, it moves or is shaped in gentle waves, like the movement of water. |

The undulating motion of the hammock made me

| modest | Someone who is modest doesn't brag about things they can do or things they have done. |

My neighbor is so modest he won't

| immune | If you are immune to something, you are not affected by it. |

Aaron is immune to chicken pox, so

| stately | Something or someone that is stately is impressive and grand in size or the way they act. |

I think horses look stately when

encumbered	If you are encumbered by something, it limits your movement or keeps you from doing what you want.

When I wear a winter coat, it encumbers me so much

that

placid	A placid person or animal is calm and doesn't get easily excited, angry, or upset.

Phillip keeps his puppy placid by

whimsical	Someone or something that is whimsical is playful and surprising.

The school play was whimsical because

endearing	If you call something a person does endearing, you mean it makes you feel fond of them.

The most endearing thing about the baby was

How Many Words Can I Use?

And still make sense!

- [ ] undulate
- [ ] modest
- [ ] immune
- [ ] stately
- [ ] encumbered
- [ ] placid
- [ ] whimsical
- [ ] endearing

Write about what you read in "Margarita's Moment." Do you like to dance? Do you know any special kinds of dancing? Do you know someone else who does? Write how you feel about dancing. Use as many words as you can. Have fun, but make sense!

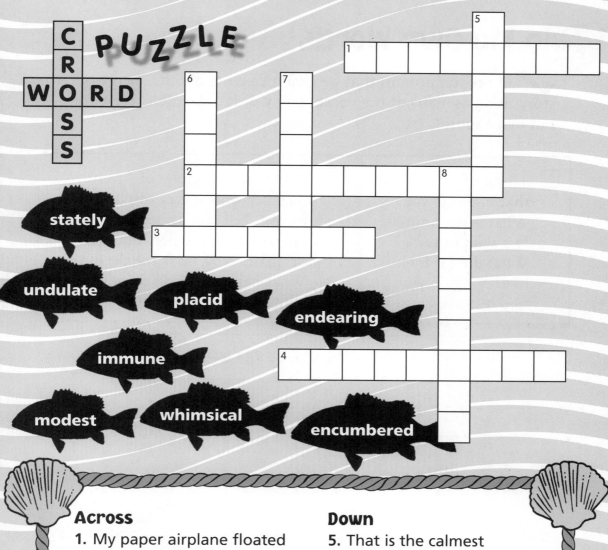

CROSS WORD PUZZLE

Word bank: stately, undulate, placid, endearing, immune, modest, whimsical, encumbered

Across

1. My paper airplane floated gently up and down before it crashed.
2. My boots are so heavy that I can barely walk.
3. I try to stand up very straight to look as grand as possible.
4. My drawing has a green sky and purple trees.

Down

5. That is the calmest bull I've ever seen!
6. I never brag about how smart I am.
7. Thanks to my earplugs, your opera music doesn't bother me.
8. I think it's so cute when Josh sneezes.

In My Own Words

Check the prompt that you want to write about. Then write a story using as many of the vocabulary words as possible. Have fun, but make sense!

☐ Think of an animal that interests you. What is the animal? Is it wild or tame? What does it look like? Why do you find it interesting?

☐ Write the biography of a family member who is very important to you. Tell about the person's life. Describe the person's looks or qualities. Who is the person? What has the person done, and why are they important?

☐ Think of your own story and write about it.

Take It Further

sufficient	If you have a sufficient amount of something, you have as much of it as you need.

Two servings of mashed potatoes and gravy are sufficient

because

mishap	If you have a mishap, something has happened to you that is bad, but not serious.

Andy had a little mishap when

defer	If you defer something, you put it off until another time or pass it off to someone else.

The group of fifth-graders decided to defer to the other group,

because

wrath	If you are experiencing someone's wrath, they are very mad at you.

Min understood his friend's wrath since

| **hilarious** | Something hilarious is very funny. |

My brother and I watched a movie that was so hilarious that

| **likeness** | If two things or people have a likeness to one another, they look a lot alike. |

My sister shares a likeness with our grandmother, but

| **dabble** | If you dabble in something, you enjoy doing it from time to time, but you aren't an expert. |

Arsalan dabbles in photography, but

| **ordeal** | An ordeal is something bad that happens that is hard to go through. |

The family next door went through a terrible ordeal when

✓ These are the words I used!

☐ sufficient
☐ mishap
☐ defer
☐ wrath
☐ hilarious
☐ likeness
☐ dabble
☐ ordeal

How Many Words Can I Use?

And still make sense!

Write about what you read in "Love That Music." Write another adventure for Danny. Where does he go? Who does he meet? Use as many words as you can. Have fun, but make sense!

VOCABULARY JUMBLE

mishap
dabble
likeness
wrath
sufficient
ordeal
defer
hilarious

The vocabulary word that best fits each clue is hidden in the jumbled letters. Find the word and connect the letters. The first one has been done for you.

L	R	R	M
A	H	L	A
S	I	L	A
U	O	I	R

1. The joke was so _____. I thought I would never stop laughing.

D	R	O	M
E	F	A	R
K	E	L	O
V	R	E	V

2. I will _____ to your decision. You have more experience than I do.

P	S	D	R
Q	O	R	D
S	L	A	E
R	M	O	C

3. I thought the camping trip would be a terrible _____, but it was actually fun.

L	E	M	I
A	A	H	S
H	P	T	C
N	O	L	O

4. I have had a _____, but it is nothing serious.

P	L	O	H
N	R	A	T
N	W	E	S
O	W	R	C

5. I was afraid of my parents' _____ after I got in trouble at school.

M	A	D	C
Z	B	B	L
O	R	S	E
L	B	B	A

6. I _____ in coin collecting, but I am not an expert.

S	U	F	F
U	L	T	I
M	R	O	C
T	N	E	I

7. I think nine hours is a _____ amount of sleep.

R	R	S	E
I	Y	S	N
Y	I	K	E
P	L	T	A

8. The _____ is amazing. I can't believe those girls are not sisters.

In My Own Words

✔ Check the prompt that you want to write about. Then write a story using as many of the vocabulary words as possible. Have fun, but make sense!

☐ Pretend that you have been granted one wish. Write a poem telling what you would wish for and why.

☐ Imagine yourself twenty years from now. What will you be doing? How will your life be different from the way it is now?

☐ Think of your own story and write about it.

☐ sufficient   ☐ defer   ☐ hilarious   ☐ dabble
☐ mishap   ☐ wrath   ☐ likeness   ☐ ordeal

19

Take It Further

capable	You are capable of doing something if you are able to do it.

I am capable of playing on a traveling soccer team because

emanate	If a sound or feeling emanates from somewhere, it comes from there.

The loud sound seemed to emanate from the kitchen, where

distinguish	If you can distinguish one thing from another, you can tell the difference between them.

People sometimes have trouble distinguishing me from my twin sister,

even though

tendency	If someone has a tendency to do something, it means they are likely to do it.

My teacher has a tendency to give less homework over the

weekend, but

| **detect** | If you detect something, you notice it or sense it, even if it is not very obvious. |

Because she can detect the slightest sound or movement, my

mother

| **mundane** | Something that is mundane is very ordinary, not at all unusual or interesting. |

The most mundane part of my morning is

| **revelation** | A revelation is a surprising or interesting fact that is made known to people. |

It was a huge revelation when

| **elicit** | If you elicit a response from a person or animal, you cause it by doing or saying something. |

Joan tried to elicit an answer from her parents by

How Many Words Can I Use?

And still make sense!

- [ ] **capable**
- [ ] **emanate**
- [ ] **distinguish**
- [ ] **tendency**
- [ ] **detect**
- [ ] **mundane**
- [ ] **revelation**
- [ ] **elicit**

Write about what you read in "Elsie and Nino."
What did you like or dislike? What surprised you?
Use as many words as you can. Have fun, but
make sense!

CROSS WORD PUZZLE

tendency
capable
detect
elicit
emanate
distinguish
mundane
revelation

Across
1. I can do it!
2. I can find anything!
3. That sound is coming from me!
4. I can tell the difference!

Down
5. This is boring!
6. I never knew that before!
7. I am likely to do it!
8. I can get a response!

23

In My Own Words

✔ Check the prompt that you want to write about. Then write a story using as many of the vocabulary words as possible. Have fun, but make sense!

☐ Think of a place other than your home where you might like to live. Where is the place? What is it like? How is it different from where you live now? Why would you like to live there?

☐ If you had one free day on which you could do anything you wanted, what would you choose to do? Write a letter to a friend about it. Describe how you would spend your day. Tell why you would choose to do those things.

☐ Think of your own story and write about it.

These are the words I used!

TOTAL WORDS USED

- [ ] capable
- [ ] distinguish
- [ ] detect
- [ ] revelation
- [ ] emanate
- [ ] tendency
- [ ] mundane
- [ ] elicit

25

Take It Further

hoist	If you hoist something heavy, you pull it or lift it up.

Gene watched the workers hoist the engine out of the car so that
they could

jubilee	A jubilee is a celebration to mark a special anniversary of an event.

The mayor of the city held a jubilee to

unremitting	If something is unremitting, it goes on and on without stopping.

The noise next door was unremitting, so

scruples	Someone's scruples are their ideas about what is fair, honest, and right.

You could tell that Felix had strong scruples because

nudge	If you nudge someone or something, you give them a gentle push, usually with an elbow.

Henry nudged me during the concert because

tranquil	If something or someone is tranquil, they are calm and peaceful.

There is nothing more tranquil than

rejuvenate	If something rejuvenates you, it makes you feel young or fresh again.

My grandfather says that being at the beach rejuvenates him

because

eccentric	An eccentric person does or says things that other people think are strange.

The scientist was a very eccentric person who

☐ hoist
☐ jubilee
☐ unremitting
☐ scruples
☐ nudge
☐ tranquil
☐ rejuvenate
☐ eccentric

How Many Words Can I Use?

And still make sense!

Write about what you read in "What's at the Movies." Which of the movies would you most want to see? Which movies would you not want to watch? Why? Use as many words as you can. Have fun, but make sense!

Hidden Clues

Fill in the blanks with the vocabulary word that best fits each clue. The letters in the boxes will spell out the answer to the question at the bottom of the page. The first one has been done for you.

1. I feel refreshed after my nap.

r e j u v e n a [t] e

2. This year's celebration is even better than last

year's celebration. __ __ __ __ __ __ [2] __

3. Will that noise ever stop?

__ __ __ __ [3] __ __ __ __ __

4. I try to do what I think is the right thing to do.

__ __ __ __ [4] __ [5] __ __ __

5. People think I'm a little strange. [6] __ __ __ __ __ __ __ __

6. I like how quiet the house is in the morning.

[7] __ __ __ __ __ __ __

7. Help me lift this box. __ [8] __ __ __

8. You elbowed me in the ribs! [9] __ __ __ __ __

nudge
eccentric
hoist
unremitting
rejuvenate
scruples
jubilee
tranquil

Who asked for the unhatched egg?

__ __ __ __ __ __ __ __ __
1   2   3   4   5   6   7   8   9

In My Own Words

✔ Check the prompt that you want to write about. Then write a story using as many of the vocabulary words as possible. Have fun, but make sense!

☐ Think about a time when you helped another person. What did you do? How did it make you feel?

☐ Have you ever been mad at someone for making too much noise? Or has someone ever been mad at you for not being quiet enough? Write a newspaper article describing a very noisy party in a town. Tell what the people in the town think about the party and the noise.

☐ Think of your own story and write about it.

Take It Further

acclaim	If you earn acclaim, you are getting public praise for something you have done.

Nick received acclaim for his voice because

curt	If you say something in a curt manner, you say it in a short, somewhat rude way.

The waiter was curt with us after

imply	If you imply something, you don't say it directly, but you let others think that is what you mean.

The neighbor implied that Peter's dog

furor	A furor is a very angry and excited reaction that people have to something.

There was a furor at our school cafeteria when

| **endow** | If someone is endowed with some special quality or ability, they have it naturally. |

James was endowed with a natural talent for

| **hamper** | If someone or something hampers you, they make it difficult for you to do what you are trying to do. |

I tried to be on time but I was hampered by

| **qualm** | If you have qualms about something, you are worried that it may be wrong in some way. |

I had qualms about going on vacation with my parents
until

| **enthralled** | If you are enthralled by something, it completely holds your attention because it is so interesting or exciting. |

Lark was enthralled by the book because

☐ acclaim
☐ curt
☐ imply
☐ furor
☐ endow
☐ hamper
☐ qualm
☐ enthralled

How Many Words Can I Use?

And still make sense!

Write about what you read in "At Home in the Rain Forest." If you could go on another trip with Dr. Smarticus, where would you want to go? Why? Use as many words as you can. Have fun, but make sense!

Word Wiggle

Fill in the boxes around the word wiggle with the vocabulary word that best fits each clue. The first one has been done for you.

1. When you say something in a short, rude way, you are being _____.

2. If someone has a special gift, they are _____ with it.

3. When someone tries to stop you from doing something, they _____ you.

4. If you earn special praise for something, you receive _____.

5. When you _____ something, you indirectly say it.

6. If you have a worry about something, you have a _____ about it.

7. When something holds you in its power, it _____ you.

8. If you are very angry about something, you are in a _____.

START

FINISH

1. c u r t

acclaim   curt
imply   furor
endowed   hamper
qualm   enthralls

In My Own Words

✓ Check the prompt that you want to write about. Then write a story using as many of the vocabulary words as possible. Have fun, but make sense!

☐ Think about someone famous who you admire for doing something brave. Write a poem about what that person did and why you think it is worthy of admiration.

☐ What are your natural gifts and talents? Write about the things you are good at, how you use them, and how you'd like to use them in the future.

☐ Think of your own story and write about it.

✔ **These are the words I used!**

- [ ] acclaim
- [ ] curt
- [ ] imply
- [ ] furor
- [ ] endow
- [ ] hamper
- [ ] qualm
- [ ] enthralled

Take It Further

melancholy	If you feel or look melancholy, you feel or look very sad.

The girl was melancholy because

insignificant	If something is insignificant, it is unimportant, usually because it is very small.

Even though the scratch looked insignificant, it

absorbed	If you are absorbed in something, you are so interested in it that it takes all your attention.

Julia was so absorbed in her book that she

dilapidated	Something that is dilapidated is old and in bad condition.

When we saw the dilapidated house, we

manipulate	If you manipulate someone, you use skill to unfairly force or convince them to do what you want.

I felt manipulated when

pompous	A pompous person acts or speaks in a way that shows they think they're more important than they really are.

The man was so pompous that

precocious	A precocious child is very smart, mature, or good at something in a way you would only expect an adult to be.

Everyone says the little girl is precocious because

scheme	A scheme is someone's plan for achieving a goal.

His scheme didn't work because

How Many Words Can I Use?

And still make sense!

- [ ] **melancholy**
- [ ] **insignificant**
- [ ] **absorbed**
- [ ] **dilapidated**
- [ ] **manipulate**
- [ ] **pompous**
- [ ] **precocious**
- [ ] **scheme**

Write about what you read in "Who Thought of That?" How do you think it would feel to invent something important? Write about how you would act if you were a successful inventor. Use as many words as you can. Have fun, but make sense!

Word Riddles

Read the clues for each number. Then fill in the blanks with the correct vocabulary word. The first one has been done for you.

absorbed
dilapidated
scheme
manipulate
insignificant
melancholy
pompous
precocious

1. insignificant
- This word describes the size of something.
- This word has five vowels.
- Something that's not a big deal is this.

2. _____
- Someone might do this to you.
- Are you trying to trick me?
- This is when you try to convince someone to do what you want.

3. _____
- This is something you make up.
- What are you plotting now?
- This is another word for a plan.

4. _____
- A way you might feel.
- Don't cry!
- This word is another way of saying you are sad.

5. _____
- This is a way someone might act.
- People might not like you if you are this.
- You are this word if you're acting like you are very important.

6. _____
- A child might be this.
- How can she do that?
- This is when a kid is good at something that usually only adults can do.

7. _____
- This is something that might happen to you.
- I wasn't paying attention.
- This is when you become interested in something and ignore everything else.

8. _____
- This is a word that describes something.
- This house is falling apart.
- This word describes something that is old and in bad condition.

In My Own Words

✔ Check the prompt that you want to write about. Then write a story using as many of the vocabulary words as possible. Have fun, but make sense!

☐ Write about a time that you had a problem and worked to solve it. How did you come up with a plan? Did it work? Why? How did you feel afterward?

☐ Do you know what it takes to be a good friend? Write a description of what you have to do and what you should not do to be a good friend.

☐ Think of your own story and write about it.

TOTAL WORDS USED

✓ These are the words I used!

- [ ] melancholy
- [ ] insignificant
- [ ] absorbed
- [ ] dilapidated
- [ ] manipulate
- [ ] pompous
- [ ] precocious
- [ ] scheme

(43)

Take It Further

| ease | If you do something with ease, it's not hard for you to do it. |

Michaela showed such ease in math class that

| propose | If you propose a plan or idea, you suggest it. |

I was surprised when our teacher proposed that we

| portable | If something is portable, it is easy to move or carry. |

The little piano is portable, so

| undertaking | If you undertake a large or difficult task, you say that you will do it. |

We knew it would be a huge undertaking, but

| penetrate | Something that penetrates something else goes into it or passes through it. |

Derrick penetrated the dark with

| durable | If something is durable, it is strong and lasts a long time. |

The box was so durable that

| indebted | If you feel indebted to someone, you are so grateful for something they did that you feel you owe them something in return. |

He felt indebted to her because

| ingenious | Something that is ingenious is very clever and original. |

Will had an ingenious idea to

How Many Words Can I Use?

And still make sense!

☐ ease
☐ propose
☐ portable
☐ undertaking
☐ penetrate
☐ durable
☐ indebted
☐ ingenious

Write about what you read in "Sports Variety Pack." What is your favorite sport? Describe the sport. Tell how you do it and why you like it. If you don't like sports, describe your favorite activity. Why is it better than sports? Use as many words as you can. Have fun, but make sense!

VOCABULARY JUMBLE

The vocabulary word that best fits each clue is hidden in the jumbled letters. Find the word and connect the letters. The first one has been done for you.

P	E	N	O
Y	N	E	T
K	M	A	R
Y	E	T	Z

1. Plunge deep into something

K	F	E	V
N	E	A	D
U	E	S	P
O	Q	I	W

2. Simple!

I	A	D	E
N	G	G	Z
I	E	N	I
H	S	U	O

3. How clever!

D	X	I	N
J	Q	E	D
W	P	B	T
V	R	D	E

4. Owed

K	S	T	L
P	R	V	H
P	O	C	D
O	S	E	G

5. Suggest

F	L	O	D
S	B	R	U
T	M	A	B
V	W	E	L

6. Strong

B	L	E	T
A	D	P	I
T	R	O	C
X	T	E	Y

7. Take it with you

I	K	A	L
N	G	T	R
U	N	D	E
B	T	Y	D

8. A big job

ease

ingenious   portable   durable   propose

penetrate   indebted   undertaking

In My Own Words

✔ Check the prompt that you want to write about. Then write a story using as many of the vocabulary words as possible. Have fun, but make sense!

☐ Think of an invention that helps you every day. Write about what it is and why you find it so useful.

☐ Pretend you are very famous and have to write an autobiography. Tell about yourself. What are the major events in your life? How have you handled your fame?

☐ Think of your own story and write about it.

These are the words I used!

- [ ] ease
- [ ] propose
- [ ] portable
- [ ] undertaking
- [ ] penetrate
- [ ] durable
- [ ] indebted
- [ ] ingenious

TOTAL WORDS USED

Take It Further

| nuzzle | If a person or animal nuzzles you, they gently rub you with their face to show they like you. |

Leah's baby brother nuzzled her cheek and

| trepidation | Trepidation is a feeling of fear about something you are going to do or experience. |

Karen had a feeling of trepidation about

| refuge | A refuge is a place you can go to be safe from something. |

Where should we find refuge if

| grapple | If you grapple with something or someone, you struggle to hold onto or control them. |

Marsha grappled with the raft, but

| ridicule | To ridicule someone or something means to make fun of them. |

Jane always ridiculed her sister about

| tempest | A tempest is a very wild and dangerous storm. |

We first heard about the tempest when

| countermand | If you countermand an instruction, you cancel it, usually by giving a new instruction. |

The head coach countermanded the assistant coach when

| luminous | Something that is luminous is bright and seems to shine or give off light. |

The lake seemed luminous because

How Many Words Can I Use?

And still make sense!

☐ nuzzle
☐ trepidation
☐ refuge
☐ grapple
☐ ridicule
☐ tempest
☐ countermand
☐ luminous

Write about what you read in "Professor Detector and the Singing Sea Serpent." What do you think Professor Detector's next case will be? How do you think she'll solve it? Use as many words as you can. Have fun, but make sense!

_____

_____

_____

_____

_____

_____

_____

_____

_____

_____

_____

_____

_____

_____

_____

_____

_____

Hidden Clues

Fill in the blanks with the vocabulary word that best fits each clue. The letters in the boxes will spell out the answer to the question at the bottom of the page. The first one has been done for you.

1. You need this if you're looking for a safe place.   r [e] f u g e

2. Your pet might get your attention this way. __ __ __ __ __ __

3. You might do this with the leash of a very excited dog.

__ __ __ __ __ [2] __

4. You would do this to someone's orders if you thought they were wrong.

__ [3] __ __ __ [4] __ __ __ __ [5]

5. A hurricane is one of these. [6] [7] [8] __ __ __ __

6. This word describes a candle. [9] __ __ __ __ [10] __ __

7. You might feel this before going to the dentist.

[11] __ __ __ __ __ __ __ __ __

8. This is a way to make fun of someone.

__ __ __ __ __ __ __ __

countermand	**grapple**	**ridicule**
trepidation	**luminous**	**refuge**
nuzzle	**tempest**	

Why did the old man care about his goats?

H __ __ __ v __ __ __ h __ __ __ __ __ s.
  1   2   3   4   5   6   7   8   9   10   11

In My Own Words

Check the prompt that you want to write about. Then write a story using as many of the vocabulary words as possible. Have fun, but make sense!

☐ Write an autobiography about the first time you remember working really hard to do something. What were you trying to do? Did you get it done? Were you happy when it was over?

☐ Have you ever had to find shelter during a storm? Where were you? Did you find a safe place to stay? Was it scary? How did you feel after the storm was over?

☐ Think of your own story and write about it.

These are the words I used!

- [ ] nuzzle
- [ ] trepidation
- [ ] refuge
- [ ] grapple
- [ ] ridicule
- [ ] tempest
- [ ] countermand
- [ ] luminous

TOTAL WORDS USED

Take It Further

weep	If you weep, you cry about a great sadness.

Ronnie didn't start weeping until

beseech	If you beseech someone, you beg them in an anxious way.

He fell to his knees and beseeched

convenient	Something that is convenient is handy because it is easy to use or works well in a particular situation.

Tiffany thought it would be more convenient to

sympathize	If you sympathize with someone, you show that you understand their feelings about something.

Eric and I sympathized with our parents about

hoax	A hoax occurs when someone creates a pretend situation and tries to make people believe it is real.

It was all a hoax when Landry

respite	If you get a respite from something you don't like, you get a short break from it.

Julia and Maria got a respite from

just	If something is just, it is fair and right.

Ted thought the umpire's decision was just, but Louisa thought

prodigious	Something that is prodigious is very large and impressive.

The building was so prodigious that it

☑ These are
the words
I used!

☐ **weep**
☐ **beseech**
☐ **convenient**
☐ **sympathize**
☐ **hoax**
☐ **respite**
☐ **just**
☐ **prodigious**

How Many Words Can I Use?

And still make sense!

Write about what you read in "Going Places." Do you like to travel? Where would you like to go? What would you do? Use as many words as you can. Have fun, but make sense!

Word Wiggle

Fill in the boxes around the word wiggle with the vocabulary word that best fits each clue. The first one has been done for you.

START

1 h o a x

2 _ _ _ _

3

4

5

9

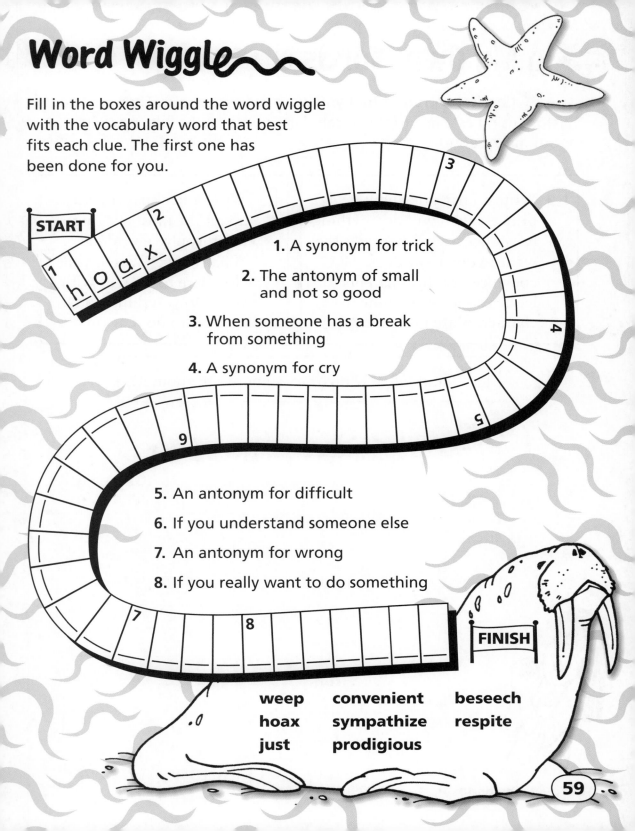

1. A synonym for trick

2. The antonym of small and not so good

3. When someone has a break from something

4. A synonym for cry

5. An antonym for difficult

6. If you understand someone else

7. An antonym for wrong

8. If you really want to do something

7

8

FINISH

weep   convenient   beseech

hoax   sympathize   respite

just   prodigious

In My Own Words

Check the prompt that you want to write about. Then write a story using as many of the vocabulary words as possible. Have fun, but make sense!

☐ Write a fairy tale about a princess who will do anything to get her way. What does she want to do? How does she convince her royal parents to let her do it? What other characters are in the story?

☐ Write a newspaper article about the most exciting thing you've ever done. What was it? Was anyone else there to share it with you? Do you think you'll ever get to do it again?

☐ Think of your own story and write about it.

Take It Further

gritty	Something that is gritty has very small pieces of stone in or on it, or feels like it does.

The floor in the room was gritty because

ailment	When you have an ailment, you are sick, but not too seriously.

Enrique's ailment made him

spur	If something spurs you on, it encourages you to start doing something or to do something faster.

Susan was spurred on to raise her grades by

vie	If you and other people vie for something, you compete with each other to get it.

The teams will vie for

jostle	If something or someone jostles you, they bump or push you in an annoying way.

Juanita was jostled when

traverse	If you traverse something, you travel over or across it.

On the way home from school, Bernard traversed

mediocre	Something that is mediocre is just okay. It's not the worst, but it's not the best either.

My handwriting is only mediocre, so

precarious	A thing or situation that is precarious is shaky and unsure. It might break down or change at any time.

The tower of blocks was precariously balanced on

☐ gritty
☐ ailment
☐ spur
☐ vie
☐ jostle
☐ traverse
☐ mediocre
☐ precarious

How Many Words Can I Use?

And still make sense!

Write about what you read in "Horse Power."
Would you like to have a pet horse? Or, would you
rather have a different kind of pet? What would
you do with your pet? Use as many words as you
can. Have fun, but make sense!

CROSS WORD PUZZLE

jostle
precarious
traverse
ailment

vie
gritty
spur
mediocre

Across

1. The cats' arrival made the pigeons hurry away.
2. That movie was okay, but not great.
3. Did you know that explorers traveled 3,700 miles to get from Missouri to Oregon?
4. My stomach hurts a little bit.

Down

5. That chair looks like it could fall over at any minute.
6. I can't believe that guy just bumped me out of the way!
7. There is sand in my shoes.
8. Our club is trying to beat Sean's club.

In My Own Words

Check the prompt that you want to write about. Then write a story using as many of the vocabulary words as possible. Have fun, but make sense!

☐ Think about a time when you competed for something. It could be an athletic event, the best grade on a test, a prize in an art contest, or anything else. Did you win? Was it fun?

☐ Write a letter to the president of the United States about a problem you'd like to see fixed. Make sure to explain why it's a problem. Offer suggestions about how to fix it.

☐ Think of your own story and write about it.

These are the words I used!

- [ ] gritty
- [ ] ailment
- [ ] spur
- [ ] vie
- [ ] jostle
- [ ] traverse
- [ ] mediocre
- [ ] precarious

TOTAL WORDS USED

67

Take It Further

| notion | A notion is an idea or belief about something. |

Celine had a notion that

| flair | If you have flair, you do things in an interesting and stylish way. |

Nanda had a lot of flair, and we could tell because

| exclusive | An exclusive place, like a club or a store, is one where only certain people are allowed to go. |

The store is so exclusive that

| swanky | If you describe a place as swanky, you mean that it is expensive and stylish. |

The swankiest place I've ever been is

| **improvise** | If you improvise, you do something without a plan and using whatever you have. |

Penelope had to improvise when

| **forte** | Something that is your forte is something you are very good at. |

Andre's forte was

| **melodious** | A melodious sound is one that is nice to listen to. |

Sasha thought the river sounded melodious because

| **lucrative** | Something that is lucrative makes you a lot of money. |

Josh's job was so lucrative that

69

☑ **These are the words I used!**

- [ ] notion
- [ ] flair
- [ ] exclusive
- [ ] swanky
- [ ] improvise
- [ ] forte
- [ ] melodious
- [ ] lucrative

How Many Words Can I Use?

And still make sense!

Write about what you read in "Meg's Forte." If you designed your own piece of art, would it be a picture, painting, or collage? What would it look like? Why? Use as many words as you can. Have fun, but make sense!

Word Wiggle

Fill in the boxes around the word wiggle with the vocabulary word that best fits each clue. The first one has been done for you.

START

1 e x c l u s i v e 2

notion
exclusive
melodious
swanky

forte
lucrative
improvise
flair

FINISH

71

In My Own Words

✓ Check the prompt that you want to write about. Then write a story using as many of the vocabulary words as possible. Have fun, but make sense!

☐ Pretend you're going to a really fancy restaurant. What will you wear? Who will you take with you? Will there be music playing in the background? What will you eat?

☐ Write about a time you got to show people something you're really good at doing. Were they impressed? How did it make you feel?

☐ Think of your own story and write about it.

These are the words I used!

- [ ] notion
- [ ] flair
- [ ] exclusive
- [ ] swanky
- [ ] improvise
- [ ] forte
- [ ] melodious
- [ ] lucrative

TOTAL WORDS USED

Take It Further

| legacy | A legacy is something special that someone leaves behind or is remembered for after they are gone. |

Emiko's grandfather left a legacy of

| mottled | Something that is mottled is covered with patches of different colors that don't make a pattern. |

The old orange was so mottled that it looked like

| retort | To retort means to reply to someone in an angry way. |

When I asked James to answer the door, he retorted,

| clamber | If you clamber somewhere, you climb there using your hands and feet because it is difficult. |

In order to get to the top, Marta had to

clamber

plummet	If something plummets, it falls a long way very quickly.

The pear plummeted toward the ground when

avarice	Someone's avarice is their greed for money and belongings.

The thief was filled with so much avarice that

moral	If you call a person or an action moral, you mean that you think they are good and right.

LaTanya thought her sister was a moral person because

confidant	If someone is your confidant, you can talk to them about anything, even private things.

Tione's confidant was her brother because

How Many Words Can I Use?

And still make sense!

- ☐ **legacy**
- ☐ **mottled**
- ☐ **retort**
- ☐ **clamber**
- ☐ **plummet**
- ☐ **avarice**
- ☐ **moral**
- ☐ **confidant**

Write about what you read in "Insects: Get the Facts!" Do you like bugs? Did you learn anything new about bugs? Do you have a favorite bug? Use as many words as you can. Have fun, but make sense!

VOCABULARY JUMBLE

The vocabulary word that best fits each clue is hidden in the jumbled letters. Find the word and connect the letters. The first one has been done for you.

G	C	M	E
N	O	H	S
F	I	W	T
K	D	A	N

1. I tell Sheri all my secrets.

E	D	W	J
L	T	T	F
A	Y	O	A
R	Y	M	P

2. This old shoe has spots all over it.

T	G	A	G
U	L	P	L
T	A	G	E
R	C	Y	D

3. My aunt left me this necklace.

M	D	S	J
O	G	F	L
R	J	D	O
A	L	T	Y

4. She is the most honest person I know.

W	K	O	G
A	T	E	S
R	O	R	L
T	J	Y	G

5. By the way he answered, I knew he was angry with me.

E	C	T	Y
S	I	R	A
R	P	H	V
F	L	O	A

6. He wanted the bicycle so badly he was ready to steal it.

C	S	Q	E
L	A	M	K
D	K	B	I
E	R	E	T

7. We climbed the hill on our hands and knees.

J	G	D	P
D	M	U	L
E	M	A	L
T	E	T	Y

8. The egg fell out of the nest so fast that it broke.

legacy
mottled moral
confidant

retort
clambered
plummeted
avarice

In My Own Words

✓ Check the prompt that you want to write about. Then write a story using as many of the vocabulary words as possible. Have fun, but make sense!

☐ Have you ever saved up money for something you really wanted? What was it? How did you earn the money? Was it difficult to be patient while you were saving?

☐ What makes someone a good person? Why do you think so? Write a biography of someone you know who is a good person. Tell about their life.

☐ Think of your own story and write about it.

Take It Further

smug	Someone who is smug is annoyingly happy about how good, smart, or lucky they are.

Sanji felt smug when he learned to

hideous	If something or someone is hideous, they are very ugly and unpleasant.

The hideous sea monsters in the movie made me

burrow	Something or someone that burrows digs through something or into something.

Charlene's pet rabbit Linus likes to burrow under

misconception	A misconception is an idea that someone believes but that is not correct.

Luisa had the misconception that

fester	A festering wound is pus-filled and infected, and the infection is usually spreading.

The cut on her elbow started to fester when

perturb	Something that perturbs you bothers you a lot.

It perturbs Vicky when her little sister

gumption	If you have the gumption to do something, you have the courage and energy to do it.

Felipe had enough gumption to

eradicate	If you eradicate something, you get rid of it completely.

Alicia planned to eradicate the weeds from her garden by

✓ **These are the words I used!**

☐ **smug**
☐ **hideous**
☐ **burrow**
☐ **misconception**
☐ **fester**
☐ **perturb**
☐ **gumption**
☐ **eradicate**

How Many Words Can I Use?

And still make sense!

Write about what you read in "Special Effects." When was the last time you wore a costume? What were you? If you were wearing a costume right now, what would it be? Use as many words as you can. Have fun, but make sense!

Hidden Clues

Fill in the blanks with the vocabulary word that best fits each clue. The letters in the boxes will spell out the answer to the question at the bottom of the page. The first one has been done for you.

1. George is convinced the world is flat.

m i s <u>c</u> <u>o</u> <u>n</u> c e p t i o n
      ¹   ²   ³

2. This cut is not getting better…and I think it's getting bigger.

__ __ __ __⁴ __ __

3. We're calling an exterminator. That will get rid of these ants!

__ __ __⁵ __ __ __ __ __ __

4. I have what it takes to do this.

__⁶ __ __ __ __ __ __ __

5. That's the ugliest thing I've ever seen!

__ __⁷ __ __ __ __ __

6. Prairie dogs live in holes underground, right?

__ __ __ __⁸ __ __

7. That annoys me. __ __ __ __⁹ __ __ __

8. I am so satisfied with myself. __¹⁰ __ __ __

hideous

smug

fester

burrow

eradicate **gumption** **misconception** **perturbs**

Why do people get warts?

Because they're __ __ __ __ __ __ __ __ __ __
          1   2   3   4   5   6   7   8   9 10

In My Own Words

Check the prompt that you want to write about. Then write a story using as many of the vocabulary words as possible. Have fun, but make sense!

☐ What is your favorite movie? Why? If you could make a sequel, what would happen?

☐ Think about a book you enjoyed reading. Who were the main characters? What was the book about? What happened in the story? Why did you enjoy it?

☐ Think of your own story and write about it.

These are the words I used!

- ☐ smug
- ☐ hideous
- ☐ burrow
- ☐ misconception
- ☐ fester
- ☐ perturb
- ☐ gumption
- ☐ eradicate

TOTAL WORDS USED

Take It Further

oblivion	Something that is in oblivion is in the situation of being unknown or not remembered.

The rocket seemed to go into oblivion when

parched	Something that is parched is very, very dry.

The plants were parched because

gallant	If you call an action gallant, someone must be brave to try it because it is dangerous and difficult.

Lawrence was very gallant during

marvel	A marvel is something that is wonderful and surprising.

The book was a marvel because

86 **Lesson 15**

| **prestigious** | If something is prestigious, people admire and respect it. |

My cousin tried out for a prestigious soccer team and

| **smirk** | If someone smirks, they smile in a mean way because they think they know more than you do. |

Raquel smirked at me because she thought

| **tribulation** | If a lot of bad things happen to you, you can say you have tribulations. |

Aaron's tribulations went on and on the day that

| **aspire** | If you aspire to something, you have a special goal that you hope to reach. |

My older sister works hard in school because she aspires to

☐ oblivion
☐ parched
☐ gallant
☐ marvel
☐ prestigious
☐ smirk
☐ tribulation
☐ aspire

How Many Words Can I Use?

And still make sense!

Write about what you read in "Edison." Did you know Thomas Edison invented those things? If you could invent anything, what would it be? Use as many words as you can. Have fun, but make sense!

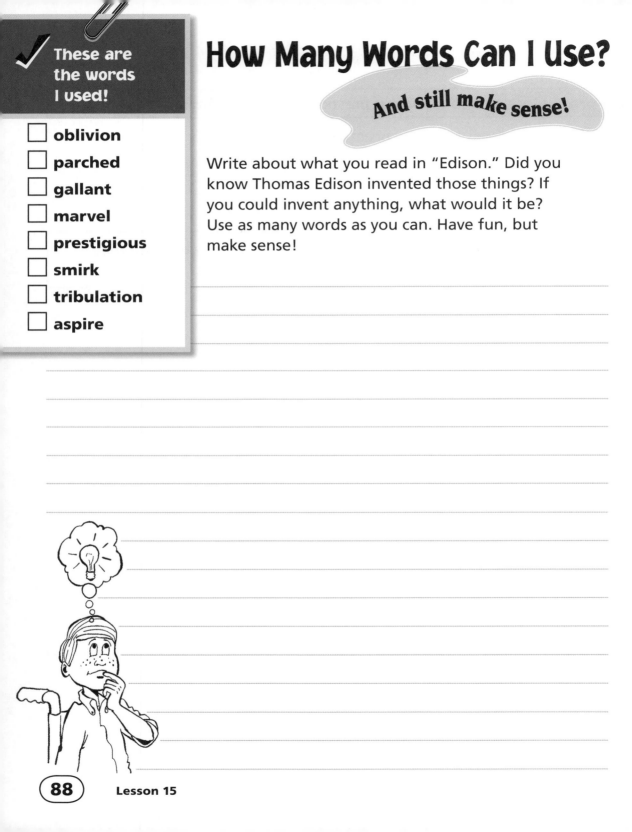

Word Riddles

Read the clues for each number. Then fill in the blanks with the correct vocabulary word. The first one has been done for you.

smirk
parched   aspire
gallant   tribulations
oblivion   prestigious
marvel

1. _marvel_
- The White House is an example of one of these.
- This word has six letters.
- A synonym for this word is a wonder.

2. _____
- This word starts with a consonant.
- This is a way to show what you're feeling.
- This is not a nice look to give someone.

3. _____
- This word has two vowels.
- This word describes most deserts.
- One synonym for this word is dry.

4. _____
- This is a description word.
- This word is about something people think is neat and important.
- This word ends with an *s*.

5. _____
- This word starts and ends with a consonant.
- One synonym for this word is brave.
- This word uses the letter *l* twice and the letter *a* twice.

6. _____
- This is something you want to do.
- This word starts and ends with a vowel.
- This describes something you hope for and work for.

7. _____
- This could describe a long road.
- This word describes something that is not around.
- This word has eight letters.

8. _____
- This word starts with a consonant.
- On good days, you don't have any of these.
- This word has every vowel except *e* in it.

89

In My Own Words

Check the prompt that you want to write about. Then write a story using as many of the vocabulary words as possible. Have fun, but make sense!

☐ Imagine you are stuck in the desert. Write a story about it. Is it hot? Are you thirsty? Is anyone with you? Does anyone else know where you are? How will you get home?

☐ Write a journal entry about something that you have not yet been able to do, but would like to do someday. What makes you want to do this? How will you feel when you reach your goal?

☐ Think of your own story and write about it.

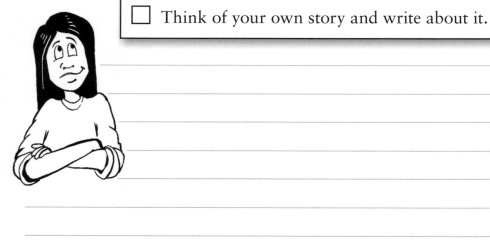

Take It Further

| patron | A patron of something is its regular customer or viewer. |

The patrons of the new TV show were thrilled because

| precede | If something precedes something else, it comes before it. |

I know that the word "apple" should precede the word "bail" in the

dictionary because

| defiance | Defiance is a way of showing you are not willing to obey someone or something. |

My sister showed a lot of defiance when

| grandeur | If something has grandeur, it is impressive because of its size, beauty, or power. |

I'd never seen a place with so much grandeur as

scornful	If you are scornful of someone or something, you show no respect for them.

Laura was scornful of the cheater because

envision	When you envision something, you picture it in your head before it actually happens.

Before I take a test, I envision myself

dismal	Something that is dismal is depressingly bad.

The field trip was a dismal failure because

legendary	If you describe someone or something as legendary, you mean that they are very famous and that many stories are told about them.

Some people might say George Washington is legendary

because

How Many Words Can I Use?

And still make sense!

☐ patron
☐ precede
☐ defiance
☐ grandeur
☐ scornful
☐ envision
☐ dismal
☐ legendary

Write about what you read in, "Who Knew?" What did you like or dislike? What surprised you? Use as many words as you can. Have fun, but make sense!

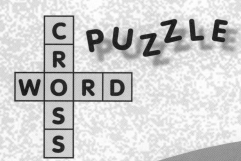

CROSS WORD PUZZLE

legendary
dismal
precedes
defiance

patrons
scornful
grandeur
envision

Across
1. Comes before something else
2. Can see it happening
3. Very well-known

Down
4. Without respect
5. Depressingly bad
6. Refusal to obey
7. Frequent customers
8. So very impressive

In My Own Words

Check the prompt that you want to write about. Then write a story using as many of the vocabulary words as possible. Have fun, but make sense!

☐ Write a story about a time when things did not go as you had planned. What went wrong? How did you feel?

☐ Would you want to meet somebody famous? Who would it be and why? What would you say?

☐ Think of your own story and write about it.

Take It Further

| resist | If you resist something, you fight against it and refuse to give in. |

Alex tried to resist jumping into the mud puddle, but

_____

_____

| vicious | If you describe something as vicious, you mean that it is mean and dangerous. |

That boy's words were vicious, so he made me feel

_____

_____

_____

| clench | When you clench something, you squeeze it tightly. |

Maria clenched her jaw because

_____

_____

_____

| accurate | If you say something is accurate, you mean that it is exactly correct. |

I thought my answer was accurate, but

_____

_____

_____

instinctive	A person or animal's action is instinctive if it comes so naturally that they do it without thinking.

The mother instinctively reached for her child when

fanciful	Something can be called fanciful if it seems like it came from someone's imagination.

The young girl wrote a fanciful story about

jeopardy	If someone or something is in jeopardy, they are in danger.

I thought I was in jeopardy when

obstruction	Something is an obstruction when it is blocking something else.

There was an obstruction in the road, so

How Many Words Can I Use?

And still make sense!

☐ resist
☐ vicious
☐ clench
☐ accurate
☐ instinctive
☐ fanciful
☐ jeopardy
☐ obstruction

Write about what you read in "Just a Little Batty." Write a review of the story. If five stars is great and one star is bad, what would you give this story? What did you like? What did you dislike? Use as many words as you can. Have fun, but make sense!

CROSS WORD PUZZLE

Word Box:
jeopardy
fanciful
instinctive
accurate
clench
obstruction
resist
vicious

Across
1. That is so dangerous!
2. That guy is so mean!
3. That is 100 percent right!
4. I did it without thinking!
5. I love to use my imagination!

Down
6. Something is in my way!
7. I won't give in!
8. I am making a fist!

In My Own Words

Check the prompt that you want to write about. Then write a story using as many of the vocabulary words as possible. Have fun, but make sense!

☐ Think about a place that you have never been and describe how you imagine it would look. Is the place real or imaginary? What do you do once you are there?

☐ Think of a problem that faces students in your school or community. Write a letter to your principal explaining the problem. What would you do to solve it? Whose help would you need to make your plan work?

☐ Think of your own story and write about it.

Take It Further

compel	If you feel compelled to do something, you feel like you have to do it for some reason.

Josie felt compelled to run when

preempt	If one thing preempts another thing, it stops it from happening, often by replacing it.

The soccer game was preempted by

endurance	Endurance is the energy to keep doing something hard for a long time.

A marathon takes a lot of endurance because

superb	Something that is superb is very, very good.

The painting was so superb that

embark	If you embark on something new and exciting, you start on it.

He couldn't embark on his trip today because

fervent	Someone who is fervent about something has strong feelings about it.

Kendra is so fervent about cats that

acclimate	When you acclimate to a new place or situation, you get used to it.

He helped me get acclimated to the cold weather by

intuitive	If someone is intuitive, they know things by having a special sense about them, even though they don't have any proof.

My aunt is intuitive about

- [ ] **compel**
- [ ] **preempt**
- [ ] **endurance**
- [ ] **superb**
- [ ] **embark**
- [ ] **fervent**
- [ ] **acclimate**
- [ ] **intuitive**

How Many Words Can I Use?

And still make sense!

Write about what you read in "It's Getting Hairy in Here." Can you think of another silly contest? What would it be? Who would compete? What would be the prize? Use as many words as you can. Have fun, but make sense!

VOCABULARY JUMBLE

The vocabulary word that best fits each clue is hidden in the jumbled letters. Find the word and connect the letters. The first one has been done for you.

intuitive
acclimate
endurance
fervent

compel
superb
embark
preempt

L	D	U	R
A	N	O	A
S	E	K	N
R	P	E	C

1. I could jump rope for hours.

R	C	C	A
I	L	O	Y
M	A	T	E
B	E	N	O

2. I am just getting used to my new school.

D	O	C	N
G	T	O	B
C	A	M	L
L	E	P	R

3. I felt a strong need to go outside.

T	M	W	O
R	E	Q	R
M	B	E	S
E	A	R	K

4. I am leaving to go on a wonderful adventure.

V	E	S	O
I	U	I	L
T	T	N	L
I	U	I	P

5. I just knew it would rain.

B	C	K	O
H	P	R	A
T	R	E	C
P	M	E	O

6. The weather report came on instead of my favorite television show.

T	H	L	E
N	R	E	F
E	V	S	T
B	L	K	Y

7. I am very serious about basketball.

B	O	R	B
K	L	E	O
Y	N	P	U
B	D	N	S

8. This is a great song.

107

In My Own Words

✔ Check the prompt that you want to write about. Then write a story using as many of the vocabulary words as possible. Have fun, but make sense!

☐ Imagine that you have done something that no one else has done before. Write a newspaper article describing what you have done. How did you do it? How did it make you feel?

☐ Think about a time you or someone you know achieved something very difficult. Write about that event or that person. What happened? How did the person act? How did everything turn out?

☐ Think of your own story and write about it.

_____

_____

_____

_____

_____

_____

_____

_____

_____

_____

_____

Take It Further

slouch	Someone who slouches lets their shoulders and head droop down in a way that doesn't look good.

The boy was slouching because

stride	Your stride is the way you walk, usually long steps you take when you're walking or running.

Macie's stride is long, so

invade	If someone invades a place, they enter it rudely or violently.

When mice invaded Lorrie's room, she

merriment	When there is merriment, people are having fun and laughing.

There was so much merriment at the fair that

| **reside** | If you reside somewhere, you live there or are staying there. |

If I could reside anywhere, I would

| **outbreak** | If there's an outbreak of something, it suddenly starts to show up in many places. |

After the outbreak of chicken pox, my school

| **symbolic** | Something that is symbolic stands for an idea or thing other than itself. |

James knew the painting was symbolic because

| **droll** | Something that is droll is funny in a smart way. |

I think Sam is droll because

How Many Words Can I Use?

And still make sense!

- [ ] slouch
- [ ] stride
- [ ] invade
- [ ] merriment
- [ ] reside
- [ ] outbreak
- [ ] symbolic
- [ ] droll

Write about what you read in "Mail Call!" Imagine you are away at camp. Write a letter home to tell what you are doing and if you are having a good time. Use as many words as you can. Have fun, but make sense!

Word Riddles

Read the clues for each number. Then fill in the blanks with the correct vocabulary word. The first one has been done for you.

1. __stride__
   - This is something you do.
   - There is a *d* in this word.
   - This is the way you walk.

2. _____
   - This word has eight letters.
   - This word sounds like the name of a musical instrument.
   - This means something that stands for something else.

3. _____
   - This is a describing word.
   - Sometimes this is a way to describe class clowns.
   - This means funny in a smart way.

4. _____
   - This word has nine letters in it.
   - What a fun time they had!
   - This word means fun and laughing.

5. _____
   - This word has three vowels.
   - It describes where you go after school.
   - It means where you live.

6. _____
   - This is something you might do.
   - Stand up straight!
   - Your head and shoulders droop.

7. _____
   - This word has two smaller words in it.
   - "It's everywhere!"
   - Something is suddenly showing up in a lot of places.

8. _____
   - This word starts and ends with vowels.
   - "What are we going to do about these mice?"
   - It means to enter rudely.

slouch   outbreak
invade   symbolic
droll   stride
reside   merriment

In My Own Words

Check the prompt that you want to write about. Then write a story using as many of the vocabulary words as possible. Have fun, but make sense!

☐ Write about a time something funny happened at school. What happened? Who saw it? How did everyone react?

☐ Think about how you walk. Do you walk fast or slow? How do you hold your head? How do your friends walk? What about clowns or movie stars? Write a poem about the different ways people walk.

☐ Think of your own story and write about it.

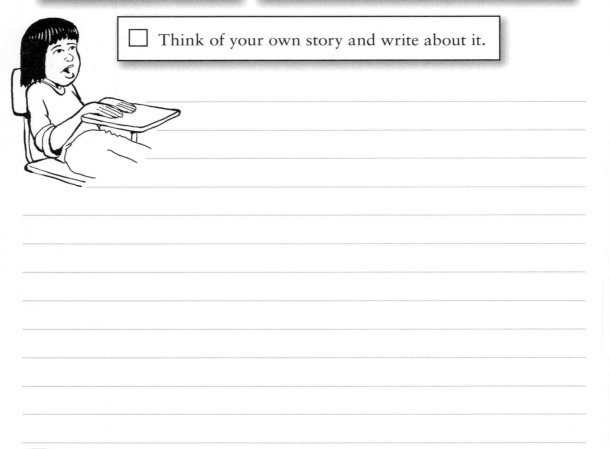

Take It Further

contraption	If you call a thing a contraption, you think it's complicated or strange, and you don't understand it or like it very much.

Eddie made a contraption that could

irresistible	If something is irresistible, you are unable to fight against it.

I find candy irresistible because

encore	An encore is a short, extra performance done at the end of a longer performance because the audience asks for more.

Kelly's band played an encore because

beckon	If you beckon to someone, you signal that you want them to come to you.

They beckoned to Anita by

mesmerize	If you are mesmerized by something, it is so amazing that you can't think of or watch anything else.

I was mesmerized by

perpetual	If something is perpetual, it goes on forever.

Cleaning up my room is perpetual because

avid	If someone is avid about something they do, they are very enthusiastic about it.

Because she was an avid runner, she

poignant	Something that is poignant affects your feelings so much that it makes you a little sad.

I thought the movie was poignant because

How Many Words Can I Use?

And still make sense!

✓ These are
the words
I used!

☐ contraption
☐ irresistible
☐ encore
☐ beckon
☐ mesmerize
☐ perpetual
☐ avid
☐ poignant

Write about what you read in "Dragons." Write another adventure for the Dragon Rescuers. What happens? What do they do? Use as many words as you can. Have fun, but make sense!

CROSSWORD PUZZLE

Across
1. I can't stay away.
2. It never stops!
3. I really, really like baseball!
4. Come here!
5. Sing one more song!

Down
6. This book made me sad.
7. What a strange machine.
8. I can't look away!

poignant
mesmerize
perpetual
encore

avid
contraption
irresistible
beckon

119

In My Own Words

✔ Check the prompt that you want to write about. Then write a story using as many of the vocabulary words as possible. Have fun, but make sense!

☐ Write a journal entry about a time when you were really interested in something. What was it? How did you learn about it? How did it make you feel? What did you like about it?

☐ Have you ever done something that seemed like it would never end? What was it? Why did it seem that way? How did you feel when it was over?

☐ Think of your own story and write about it.

These are the words I used!

- [ ] contraption
- [ ] irresistible
- [ ] encore
- [ ] beckon
- [ ] mesmerize
- [ ] perpetual
- [ ] avid
- [ ] poignant

TOTAL WORDS USED

Take It Further

| restricted | If something is restricted, it is limited to a certain place, size, or group of people. |

The room was restricted to

| stash | If you stash something, you put it in a safe, secret place. |

Josh stashed his *mom's* birthday present in

| meld | If you meld two or more things, you combine them or blend them together. |

Sacha made a snack by melding

| consult | If you consult someone, you get advice or information from them. |

Hans decided to consult his teacher about

gadget	A gadget is a small machine or device that does something useful.

Lucita wants a gadget that can

scout	If you scout for something, you search for it, often in a certain area.

We scouted for berries by

surmise	If you surmise something, you guess that it's true based on what you know, but you don't know for sure.

Because it was cloudy, Lily surmised that

plausible	If you say something is plausible, you think that it could reasonably be true.

His excuse seemed plausible, so

How Many Words Can I Use?

And still make sense!

Write about what you read in "Joke Match." Which jokes were your favorites? Why? Do you have any other favorite jokes? Try writing your own joke. Use as many words as you can. Have fun, but make sense!

Word Wiggle

Fill in the boxes around the word wiggle with the vocabulary word that best fits each clue. The first one has been done for you.

1. A digital camera is one of these.
2. An artist does this when mixing paints.
3. Dogs and cats usually aren't allowed in restaurants.
4. I went first to check stuff out.
5. You would do this if you needed to learn something from somebody.
6. The newspaper story sounded true.
7. When you want to hide something, you do this.
8. You can guess what will happen next.

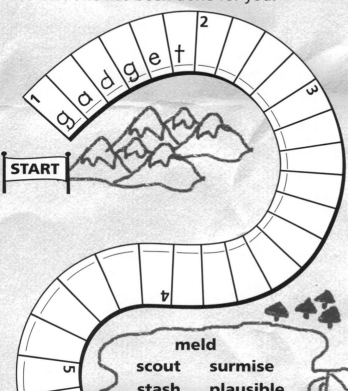

1 g a d g e t 2

3

START

4

5

meld
scout   surmise
stash   plausible
consult   gadget
restricted

6

7

FINISH

8

N

125

In My Own Words

✔ Check the prompt that you want to write about. Then write a story using as many of the vocabulary words as possible. Have fun, but make sense!

☐ Write about a time when you got a new toy. Describe it. How often did you play with it at first? Did you let anyone else play with it? Do you still play with it?

☐ Think of something you'd really like to learn about. What do you know about it already? Who would you talk to if you wanted to find out more about it? What questions would you like answered about this subject?

☐ Think of your own story and write about it.

Take It Further

yearn	If you yearn for something, you want it very much.

Taylor yearned to

limelight	If you are in the limelight, you are getting a lot of public attention.

I was put in the limelight when

flail	Something that is flailing is waving around wildly.

Until Brian learned to dance, his arms flailed like

verge	If you are on the verge of something, you are about to do it or ready to do it.

Aieko was on the verge of

mingle	If people or things mingle, they mix together and interact with each other.

At the party, it was fun to mingle with people because

feign	If you feign something, you pretend to feel it or do it.

Nia's brother feigned being asleep so that

incessant	Something that is incessant keeps happening and never stops.

The incessant sound of the water dripping off the roof made me

want to

miserable	If someone or something is miserable, they are very unhappy or they make you feel very unhappy.

Jose felt miserable because

☑

□ yearn
□ limelight
□ flail
□ verge
□ mingle
□ feign
□ incessant
□ miserable

How Many Words Can I Use?

And still make sense!

Write about what you read in "The Worst Vacation Ever!" Have you ever thought something would be boring, only to end up having fun? Write about it. Use as many words as you can. Have fun, but make sense!

Hidden Clues

Fill in the blanks with the vocabulary word that best fits each clue. The letters in the boxes will spell out the answer to the question at the bottom of the page. The first one has been done for you.

1. Something that never stops i n [c] e s s [a] n t

2. Fake something [_] __ __ __ __

3. Someone who is very sad __ __ __ [_] __ __ __ __ __

4. Public attention __ __ __ __ __ __ __ __ [_]

5. To mix together at a party __ __ __ __ __ [_]

6. When you are about ready to do something __ __ [_] __ __

7. Wave your arms all around __ __ __ [_] __

8. You really want something __ __ [_] __ __

limelight   yearn   flail   miserable   mingle   incessant   verge   feign

The talent show was held in the __ __ __ __ __ __ __ __ __
$\quad\quad$ 1 2 3 4 5 6 7 8 9

131

In My Own Words

✔ Check the prompt that you want to write about. Then write a story using as many of the vocabulary words as possible. Have fun, but make sense!

☐ Write a story about the last time you were embarrassed. When was it? Why did it happen? Did you expect to feel embarrassed?

☐ Think about someone whose talents you admire. What makes them special? Do you want to try to do the same things they do? Why or why not?

☐ Think of your own story and write about it.

Take It Further

lean	Someone or something that is lean is thin and doesn't have a lot of extra fat or weight.

My cat is very lean, so

listless	If you are listless, you have no energy and don't feel like doing anything.

I feel listless today because

animation	Someone with animation is lively in the way they act or speak.

Gretchen spoke with animation when

reticent	If you are reticent, you are shy and do not like to share your thoughts and feelings with others.

The boys are reticent, but

| **magnitude** | The magnitude of something is its large size or importance. |

The magnitude of the building surprised me because

| **conspicuous** | If something or someone is conspicuous, they stick out and are very obvious. |

He felt conspicuous when

| **esteem** | If you feel esteem for someone, you admire and respect them. |

Jordan held his grandmother in esteem because

| **gregarious** | If you are gregarious, you enjoy being with other people. |

Cheyenne is usually gregarious, but

✓ **These are the words I used!**

- [ ] lean
- [ ] listless
- [ ] animation
- [ ] reticent
- [ ] magnitude
- [ ] conspicuous
- [ ] esteem
- [ ] gregarious

How Many Words Can I Use?

And still make sense!

Write about what you read in "Racer Miles—Secret Video Game Tester." Think about the things you are good at. Would you like to have a secret job doing any of those things? What would you do? Would it be hard not to tell your friends? Use as many words as you can. Have fun, but make sense!

VOCABULARY JUMBLE

The vocabulary word that best fits each clue is hidden in the jumbled letters. Find the word and connect the letters. The first one has been done for you.

lean
esteem
listless
reticent

animation
magnitude
conspicuous
gregarious

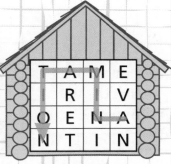

T	A	M	E
R	I	V	N
O	E	N	A
N	T	I	N

1. I am full of energy!

R	E	C	L
E	T	M	T
K	I	S	T
P	C	E	N

2. I'm not telling!

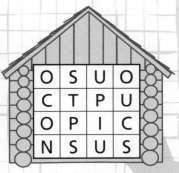

O	S	U	O
C	T	P	U
O	P	I	C
N	S	U	S

3. I stick out!

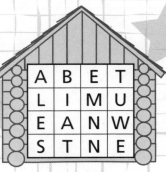

A	B	E	T
L	I	M	U
E	A	N	W
S	T	N	E

4. I'm skinny!

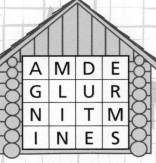

A	M	D	E
G	L	U	R
N	I	T	M
I	N	E	S

5. I look big and important!

S	U	O	I
S	T	N	R
E	V	P	A
G	R	E	G

6. I really like being around people!

B	C	P	Y
L	I	O	S
E	S	T	S
A	I	L	E

7. I'm not really interested.

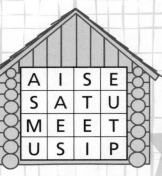

A	I	S	E
S	A	T	U
M	E	E	T
U	S	I	P

8. I think you're great!

(137)

In My Own Words

Check the prompt that you want to write about. Then write a story using as many of the vocabulary words as possible. Have fun, but make sense!

☐ If you could meet someone from history, who would you choose to meet? Why would you want to meet them? What would you ask them? What would you do with them?

☐ Write a poem about your friends. What are they like? How are they the same or different than you?

☐ Think of your own story and write about it.

Take It Further

quip	To quip means to say something that you intend to be funny and clever.

Tamaan makes a lot of quips, so

attire	Your attire is the clothes you are wearing.

Paul decided that the best attire for the dance would be

subside	If a condition subsides, it gets less serious and begins to go away.

I hoped that my cold would subside so

intent	If you are intent on something, you concentrate very hard on it.

Annick was so intent on learning piano that

burden	A burden is a heavy load or something that causes you a lot of worry or work.

Instead of thinking of her chores as a burden, Sarah

foreboding	If you feel foreboding, you feel like something very bad is going to happen.

She felt a strong sense of foreboding right before

solace	Something that is a solace comforts you and makes you feel less sad.

When things weren't going well, James found great solace in

heed	If you heed something or someone, you pay attention to them or what they say.

Fred decided to heed his mother's warning and

How Many Words Can I Use?

And still make sense!

- [ ] **quip**
- [ ] **attire**
- [ ] **subside**
- [ ] **intent**
- [ ] **burden**
- [ ] **foreboding**
- [ ] **solace**
- [ ] **heed**

Write about what you read in "It Takes All Kinds."
Did you agree with your results? Why or why not?
Use as many words as you can. Have fun, but
make sense!

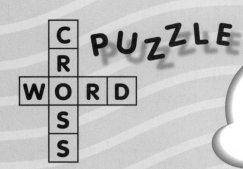

CROSS WORD PUZZLE

solace
quip
burden
intent

subside
foreboding
heed
attire

Across
1. You do this when you want to make people laugh.
2. It doesn't look good.
3. This is how you are dressed.
4. You'd better listen to my advice.

Down
5. Something that becomes less and less.
6. If you were this, it would be difficult to get your attention.
7. This is a pain to carry around.
8. This will make you feel better.

In My Own Words

Check the prompt that you want to write about. Then write a story using as many of the vocabulary words as possible. Have fun, but make sense!

☐ Write about a time when you thought something bad might happen. What was it? Did it end up happening after all? Was there anything you could do to stop it?

☐ Write about a favorite book that makes you feel comfortable and safe. Where do you go to read it? What is it about? Why does it make you feel better?

☐ Think of your own story and write about it.

Words I Have Learned

A

absorbed
acclaim
acclimate
accurate
ailment
animation
arresting
aspire
attire
avarice
avid

B

beckon
beseech
burden
burrow

C

capable
clamber
clench
compel
composure
confidant
conspicuous
consult
contract
contraption

convenient
countermand
curt

D

dabble
defer
defiance
detect
dilapidated
dismal
distinguish
droll
durable

E

ease
eccentric
elicit
emanate
embark
encore
encumbered
endearing
endow
endurance
enthralled
envision
eradicate
esteem
exclusive

F

fanciful
feign
fervent
fester
flail
flair
foreboding
forte
furor

G

gadget
gallant
grandeur
grapple
gregarious
gritty
gumption

H

hamper
heed
hideous
hilarious
hoax
hoist

I

immune
imply
improvise
impulse
incessant
indebted
infer
ingenious
insignificant
instinctive
intent
intuitive
invade
irresistible

J

jeopardy
jostle
jubilee
just

L

lean
legacy
legendary
likeness
limelight
listless
lucrative
luminous

M

magnitude
manipulate
marvel
mediocre
melancholy
meld
melodious
merriment
mesmerize
mingle
misconception
miserable
mishap
modest
moral
mottled
mundane

N

notion
nudge
nuzzle

O

oblivion
obstruction
ordeal
outbreak

P

parched
patron
penetrate
perceptive
perpetual
perturb
placid
plausible
plummet
poignant
pompous
portable
precarious
precede
precocious
preempt
prestigious
prodigious
propose

Q

qualm
quip

R

refuge
refute
rejuvenate
reside
resist
respite
restricted

reticent
retort
revelation
ridicule

S

scheme
scornful
scout
scruples
slouch
smirk
smug
solace
spirited
spur
stash
stately
stride
subside
sufficient
superb
surmise
swanky
symbolic
sympathize

T

tempest
tendency
tranquil
traverse
trepidation
tribulation

U

undertaking
undulate
unremitting

V

verge
vicious
vie

W

weep
whimsical
wrath

Y

yearn

Highlight your favorite words!

Other Favorite Words

You learn new words every day. Some of them you will always want to remember. Here is a place to write down words you learn from other places!

I

heard   saw   used

(circle one)

this word: _____.

Where and how: _____

_____

I

heard   saw   used

(circle one)

this word: _____.

Where and how: _____

_____

I

heard   saw   used

(circle one)

this word: _____.

Where and how: _____

_____

I

heard   saw   used

(circle one)

this word: _____.

Where and how: _____

_____

I

heard   saw   used

(circle one)

this word: _____.

Where and how: _____

_____

I

heard   saw   used

(circle one)

this word: _____.

Where and how: _____

_____

Word
Watcher

Word
Watcher

Word
Watcher

Word
Watcher

Word
Watcher

Word
Watcher